Is It Really Love?

by

Ken Stewart, D. Min.

KEN STEWART MINISTRIES, INC.
P. O. BOX 35382
TULSA, OKLAHOMA 74135

HARRISON HOUSE
P.O. Box 35035
Tulsa, Okla. 74135

(All Scripture quotations from *King James version* of the Bible, unless otherwise stated.)

A new commandment I give unto you, That ye love one another; as I have loved you, that ye also love one another.—John 13:34

ISBN 089274-077-9
Copyright © 1978 by Ken Stewart Ministries, Inc.
Printed in the United States of America
All rights reserved

INTRODUCTION

Many books have been written on the subject of love. Yet, the percentage of people who really grasp the meaning of love is very small. This is true even of those who claim to base their lives totally on the Word of God.

I believe this can and must be changed. You can understand the true meaning of love. It is not a great hidden mystery still waiting to be discovered. God has revealed to us in His Word what love really is. We need only to take a serious look at the Scriptures to grasp its meaning for us.

Too much of the time we listen to what others have to say about love rather than going by what God has said about it. Obviously this is the reason for the vast misunderstanding of the subject. We need to understand what love really is. Then we must learn to be consistent in expressing love to others even when we do not anticipate it working to our advantage.

Love demands action. Inactive love is really not love in any sense of the word. Love will always demand action. And, eventually love will draw a re-action.

The principle of love taught in the Word of God is to give love and it will be given unto you. That is what God did in giving His only begotten Son to die for the sins of man. He gave love and He receives love in return. I John 4:19 states it like this, "We love Him, because He first loved us." We must learn to follow His example.

Obviously, not everyone that God loves, responds with love. In fact, He has loved many who have never acknowledged Him. But, He keeps on loving. There may be many people who will spurn your love even as they do the love of God. Keep following His example. Keep on loving. In your own home, keep on loving. In your church, keep on loving. In your neighborhood, keep on loving. In your office, or school, or prison cell, keep on loving. No matter where you are, keep on loving. God does, and because He does, you can.

Several years ago I listened to a series of tapes by C. S. Lewis. He spoke of "The Four Loves." As I have meditated on the Word of God, I have recalled a few of his comments and have discovered the truth I want to share with you.

I am grateful to the Holy Spirit for His illumination of the Word of God. Indeed, He is responsible for anything of value I have to share. May all the glory and praise go to our Father who is love.

IS IT REALLY LOVE?

EPHESIANS 5:22-33

22 Wives, submit yourselves unto your own husbands, as unto the Lord.

23 For the husband is the head of the wife, even as Christ is the head of the church: and he is the saviour of the body.

24 Therefore as the church is subject unto Christ, so let the wives be to their own husbands in everything.

25 Husbands, love your wives, even as Christ also loved the church, and gave himself for it;

26 That he might sanctify and cleanse it with the washing of water by the word.

27 That he might present it to himself a glorious church, not having spot, or wrinkle, or any such thing; but that it should be holy and without blemish.

28 So ought men to love their wives as their own bodies. He that loveth his wife loveth himself.

29 For no man ever yet hated his own flesh; but nourisheth and cherisheth it, even as the Lord the church:

30 For we are members of his body, of his flesh, and of his bones.

31 For this cause shall a man leave his father and mother, and shall be joined unto his wife, and they two shall be one flesh.

32 This is a great mystery: but I speak concerning Christ and the church.

33 Nevertheless let every one of you in particular so love his wife even as himself; and the wife see that she reverence her husband.

As we look at the subject of love please notice immediately in verse 22 of the above Scripture passage, the comparison between *husbands and wives,* and *Christ and the church.*

God has chosen the marriage relationship to give man a clear understanding of the relationship Christ should have with the church. Obviously, He had something very different in mind to what we see in most marriages today. I have done a great deal of marriage counselling, and there are so many people who are getting a divorce these days. I don't know about you, but I am alarmed by that.

What alarms me is how much born-again, Spirit-filled believers have bought what the world has to say about marriage, and what the world has to say about love, and about divorce. We've got a problem somewhere. We as Christians — as born-again, Spirit-filled believers have gotten our ideas about marriage and about love from the world. And really, when you stop and think about it, what does this old world know about love?

I believe that the answer is obvious from what the world does: they know absolutely nothing about love. They have proven over, and over, and over again that they DO NOT KNOW WHAT LOVE IS! This is the reason that we have so many broken homes. This is the reason that we have child abuse. This is the reason that we have so many divorces. This is the reason that we have so many couples living together who are not married: simply because these people understand nothing about love.

A BLANKET STATEMENT

I am going to make a very straight-forward, blanket statement that may surprise you. *Those who are not born-again do not know what love is,* and no matter how long they have been married, *they do not have real love if they don't have JESUS!*

Oh — they *say* that they love, that they know what love is, and that's why they got married. But they have proven over, and over that they don't know what love is, because they stay married forty-eight hours and get a divorce, or forty-eight years and get a divorce.

Why?

Because they don't have love, and that is the reason that I am talking to you about what love really is.

ASSUMPTIONS WE CANNOT AFFORD—

We *assume* that families love each other. We are all part of a family and we are supposed to love everybody in our family. We act like we think love is automatic, just because that's Mother, just because that's Daddy, just because that's Brother, or just because that's Sister. Just because that's Grandma or Grandpa or Son or Daughter — we *assume* that they love us no matter what. Just because she is my wife I *assume* that she loves me and that she knows that I love her. Just because he is your husband you may *assume* that he loves you and that he knows that you love him. *These are assumptions that we cannot afford.* I said, "THESE ARE ASSUMPTIONS THAT WE CANNOT AFFORD!"

The divorce rate and the rate at which homes are falling apart, even supposedly Christian homes should be proof enough: we cannot assume love any more. In fact, I believe one of the greatest mistakes that is being made today is in taking one another *for granted.*

Husbands, wives, parents, and children, remember this: ASSUMPTIONS ARE ALMOST ALWAYS MADE FOR THE ADVANTAGE OF THE ONE DOING THE ASSUMING! I *assume* that you love me because it is advantageous to me to make that *assumption.* I don't have to put out so much. I don't have to be so conscientious in the way I act if I can just *assume* that you love me. I don't have to make such a great effort to behave myself as I should, to act as I should, to respond to you as I should, if I can just assume that you love me. As I said, *"assumptions are almost always made for the advantage of the one doing the assuming."* And I don't believe that we can *assume love* any longer.

WE NEED MORE LOVE IN THE HOME —

It seems strange to say it, but we need more love in the home. When we think of a home we think of love, and we automatically attach the two together. We just sort of think that if there's a home there is love. And obviously that is not the case.

I am going to try to show you something through this book, and I am going to speak rather plainly in doing it. Follow me and I believe that it will help you. If you are married, it will help your marriage. If you are not, it will certainly help you when you do get married.

The first thing that God did when He created man was to start a family. In Genesis, chapter 2, and verse 18, we read; "And the Lord God said, It is not good that the man should be alone; I will make him an help meet for him." God put families before the plan of salvation. Before He ever developed the nation of Israel, He developed a family. In fact, that's how the nation of Israel came about. We would not have a Saviour if it were not for a family. It was a Son born into a family that brought the Saviour into this world.

GOD'S NUMBER ONE EXAMPLE —

God has attempted to show the world what His relationship is like with the Church, and the number one example that He has given to us is the family. That's what the Word says in Ephesians chapters five and six. The family is God's idea. I said, "The family is God's idea."

Since the very beginning the devil has been trying to destroy the family. He started with one brother killing another, in an effort to destroy the first family but he could not do it. He hasn't done it and he won't do it! Because the family is God's idea.

This business of couples living together is the devil's idea. Lesbianism, homosexualism is the devil's idea. I don't care what church, and what bishop endorses it. God does not endorse it. He never has and He never will. God started the family and it is up to us to decide whether we'll help God keep the family together or help the devil tear it apart.

THE GREEKS HAD FOUR WORDS FOR "LOVE" —

Now there are four kinds of *love*. In English we just say, "Love." And that means so many different things that we never know for sure what we are talking about. In the same conversation we say, "I love bananas and I love my wife:" or "I love peanutbutter and I love my children:" or "I love puppy dogs and I love you." But it wasn't so with the Greeks. They used four different words for *love: Agape, phileo, storge,* and *eros.*

AGAPE: That's the highest kind of love. *Agape* means a love which comes from realizing and understanding the value and preciousness of a person. The quality of this love is determined by the character of the one who loves and the person loved. *Agape* is the God kind of love. He realizes and understands how precious you are, and the character of this love, or the quality of this love I should say, is determined by the character of God. I said, *"It is determined by the character of the one who loves and the person who is loved."* That means — where your character is lacking in this love His character makes up the difference. That's *agape*.

PHILEO: *Phileo* means "friend." *Phileo* is a love consisting of whatever we see in a person that gives us pleasure. *Phileo's* quality is determined by the character of the one who loves and the one loved, but it is extended on the basis of pleasure — not character. Thus, people have the wrong friends. And where two people of very low character get together, they can be friends all right, but the level and measure of love is very low and very poor.

STORGE: *Storge* is the third word for love. *Storge* simply means affection. This is the kind of love most often shown by the world to children, to the elderly, and to each other. *Storge* may or may not take any account of the individual. It's that momentary pat on the head, a smile, a handshake, a hug, even a kiss that may mean nothing.

Storge combined with *agape* can be meaningful. But *storge* combined with *phileo* without *agape* can lead to number four (*eros*).

EROS: *Eros* is sex. *Eros* also means sexual attraction without the act of sex. This is the kind of love that the world would have us believe is the highest level — the highest kind of love. *Eros* very often occurs between those without character outside of marriage. But *eros* can only take on its true meaning when it is combined with *agape* in the marriage relationship. It is only in the marriage relationship that you can have the combination of *agape* and *eros,* because you can only see a person as valuable and precious in a sexual relationship in a marriage.

Now this is a very quick treatment of these four Greek words (*agape, phileo, storge,* and *eros*), but I believe that it will suffice for what I have to point out to you. Think about these four kinds of love with me through the following example: Boy meets girl. Boy is a Christian. Girl is a Christian. Both were raised in Christian homes. Both go to church, in fact they met at church. Boy dates girl. Days go by. Date after date, then boy and girl decide one day, "We're in love!"

Why?

"Why? Nobody ever asks why. We are in love."

Why do you think you are in love?

"Well, because we've been dating for about three weeks. We've eaten pizza together. We like the same kind of chewing gum. She likes my car. I like her perfume and she likes my aftershave. And beside that, she turns me on and I turn her on, so we're getting married. We are in love."

What kind of love?

"Oh, love!"

No — what kind of love? Peanut-butter love? Banana love? Or the kind of love that lasts for sixty years? What kind of love?

THE PHILEO LEVEL —

A dating relationship usually begins on the *phileo level*. That of friends. They give each other pleasure.

They enjoy each other's company. They are friends. He's nice. She's nice. She's good-looking. He's handsome. Maybe it is because he drives a nice car. Who knows? But they give each other pleasure.

Agape should be the reason that they are dating but that doesn't happen very often. Usually it is *phileo*.

THE STORGE LEVEL —

They begin as friends, and it isn't long until *storge* enters the picture. It used to be a question as to whether or not a girl would accept a kiss on the first date. Now there is no question: it's when he picks her up at the front door. There is holding hands and kissing and hugging. You see, *storge* has entered the picture.

PHILEO AND STORGE GET INVOLVED WITH EROS —

We now have *phileo* and *storge,* and before you know it *eros* is involved. At the level of sexual attraction that is. At that level *eros* is not a sin because men are men and women are women. But if it goes further than that, it becomes a sin.

AGAPE: IMPORTANT AND NECESSARY —

Parents, the reason that there are so many young people living together without getting married is because we have taught them so little about *agape*. They begin as friends; *storge* gets involved. You add *storge* to *phileo* and *eros* is the result — if you don't have *agape*.

We have not taught boys to see girls as valuable and precious, and we have not taught girls to see boys as valuable and precious. We have not taught people to see people as valuable and precious. Therefore when you combine *storge* with *phileo,* you have *eros:* then you have couples living together without getting married.

You cannot understand and realize the value and preciousness of someone and enter into premarital sex with them. The very thing itself says, "I don't see you as having any value." I know that's blunt, but it needs to be.

Back to the dating now. It begins with *phileo* — pleasure: *storge* — affection: And, if marriage does not occur at this point and there is no *agape*, then as this level of combination of *storge* and *phileo* is maintained — *eros* is inevitable, especially if we have a dating relationship between those who do not know the Lord. If they do not know the Lord they are essentially void of *agape*. *Eros* is also inevitable if we have a dating relationship between one who is a Christian and one who is not, because half of that relationship is essentially void of *agape*.

What is surprising is that even among this generation when the Word of God is being taught and preached so forcefully, there are couples where both are Christians, and their dating relationship is still void of *agape*.

Why?

Because they have not been taught that particular thing (agape).

PHILEO CAN GO OUT THE WINDOW —

If a marriage does occur between a couple without *agape*, I want you to understand that it can work as long as they continue to find each other pleasing in some way. That is the *phileo* level of love. But when he gets bald and she gets fat, and the battle of the bulge begins, *phileo* goes out the window. As long as they appreciate each other's affection or as long as the sexual adjustment is adequate, couples may remain married. In the past they have remained married without any of those *(agape, storge, phileo, or eros)*, simply because of social pressure. But that social pressure has been relieved and it has shown us the rottenness of the relationship that there is between husbands and wives who do not know the Lord. So we have divorces between couples who have been married for forty and fifty years. It simply screams that for forty years there has been no love in that home.

SATAN IS AT WORK —

There are almost enough pressures without Satan, in fact to guarantee disaster. Without *agape* a marriage is bound to wind up in divorce. If you do not value your lifetime partner, it is easy — later on to find someone else that you think will please you more. Satan has done a dandy job in turning sacred things into common things and perverting the minds of men and women.

I ask you this question. What kind of love do you have?

If you say, "Oh, it doesn't matter, we are in love. We are Christians and we are in love, and we will make it. God will see to it."

Don't kid yourself. *If you don't see to it, God can't.*

Some couples get married and even though they are both Christians, and have experienced *agape*, that does not mean that they have *agape* for each other. *Agape* isn't automatic. Just because you have experienced God's love that does not mean that you have *agape* love for someone else.

They have *eros*, they have *storge*, she kisses nice, they have *phileo*. They see something in each other besides sex that gives them pleasure. She is a good cook, and he has a good job, but in most cases they don't have *agape*.

AGAPE TAKES TIME —

Do you know why they don't have *agape?*

Because *agape* takes *time.* It takes *effort.* It takes *work on your selfishness.* It takes *patience* to see somebody else as *valuable* and *precious.*

Remember this, single people: you have a much better chance of developing *agape* before marriage than you do after.

"Why?"

Because when sex has gotten old, when his kisses have gotten cold, when her cooking has collected mold, it's hard to take time and make the effort to begin to realize and understand the value and preciousness of that wonderful gal or guy that you married.

THE STARTING PLACE —

You say, "Well, what about those that are already married?"

Well, if the luster has gone out of your marriage, then work on *agape.* Start looking for something *valuable* and *precious* in that person that you are married to.

You say, "I don't see anything. . . ."

Wait a minute! God does! And if He can see something *valuable* and *precious* in your husband or wife, then you can. There's the place to begin. Start with your husband or wife, and then do the same with your children.

You can't base a home on *eros*.

You can't base a home on *storge*.

You can't base a home on *phileo*.

You can only build a home on *agape*. The home that is built on *agape* is a real home: the kind of home that children bring the grandchildren home to.

So many times couples meet and they are friends, and they should be. They should always be friends, but that's not enough. They soon become affectionate friends and it should always be that way, but that's not enough. They get married, and then they are affectionate friends with a sexual relationship that is ordained and approved by God, but that's not enough.

AGAPE IS A "MUST" —

Children are born and immediately there are problems in the home.

"Why?"

Because you can't look at your children as friends. That's why. A six month old baby crying in the middle of the night does not make a very good friend. You certainly can't approach that child in love, on the basis of *eros*. That is obvious.

You say, "Well, that's *phileo,* and that's *eros*. What about *storge?*"

Well, that gets old too! To you and to that two and a half year old child who wipes your kisses off his cheek and starts throwing temper tantrums. There has to be *agape*. You have got to be involved in your home, in your marriage, in your family because you see this wife, this husband, this child, as valuable and precious. If that's not where you are coming from you won't stay, because society has decided to let you out.

If *agape* is not there, that child grows, and the parents try the other kinds of love, and none of them work, so the child rebels and runs away.

The constant cry is, "If my parents only saw me as somebody." So many teenagers have looked me in the eye and said, "If my parents could only see that I'm somebody, that I am worth something." They have set out to prove that they are worth something. They have set out to convince their parents.

And what do you hear their parents saying?

"It's almost like my kids are trying to prove something." HEY! WAKE UP. THEY ARE! They are trying to prove to you that they are somebody, that they are worth something, that they are valuable. *That somebody thinks that they are valuable.*

When that fifteen or sixteen year old girl walks into your living room and says, "I'm getting married to this guy that you think is a clod." just remember that she is saying to you, "I've found somebody who thinks that I am worth something."

That is what it's all about. Maybe they still haven't found *agape*. If you haven't given *agape* love to them in the home, they probably haven't found it somewhere else.

You see, people are people, and people are what makes a home. People are valuable and precious. In fact, God gave His only begotten Son, just because He sees people as valuable and precious.

But yet — men and women see so little value and so little preciousness in their own families, that they are willing to walk out the door and slam it in their faces and say, "Make it the best way you can. I'll go my own selfish way. I am worth more than you are."

That has never pleased God and it never will.

SO — YOU'VE BEEN DIVORCED —

You say, "Well, I've already gone through divorce. My home is already split. I am married again now." Or, "I am contemplating marriage again." This may be the second marriage for you, or the third one, or maybe even the fourth one: whatever. And you may ask, "What do you say about that?"

Well: If you have not approached those marriages in the past with *agape,* don't make the same mistake again. The same mistake will bring the same result again. It seems only reasonable to think that if you have experienced the hurt and the pain of the break-up of one home and one marriage, you wouldn't want that to happen again. It seems reasonable that your number one desire would be to approach this marriage right. And, I am telling you what's right — *agape*. AGAPE.

If you cannot look at that person whom you are dating, and that you are contemplating marriage with, as valuable and precious, then YOU HAD BETTER NOT MARRY HER, or HIM. If you can't look at that person as valuable and precious before marriage, when you find out what he or she is really like after marriage, you sure can't do it then. That's a fact.

DO SOMETHING ABOUT IT NOW —

If you are already married and there are problems in your home, problems in your relationship, then I have a word for you. *"Do something about it."*

You may ask, "What can I do about it? How do I do something about it? We have always had problems! We have always fought since the night that we got married. What can we do about it? What is the key?"

AGAPE! God gave it to you. Are you going to be selfish enough not to give it to that person to whom you are married?

Freely you have received. Freely give. I am talking about *agape*. Realize and understand the value and preciousness of your home. Realize and understand the value and preciousness of the persons in your home. If it takes it — if you have to, get on your face before God and say, "God, show me something valuable and precious about this individual I am married to." There is nothing wrong with that. I will promise you one thing. If you do this you will get up from your knees and look at your husband or wife differently. Even if there are no problems in your home, it would be a good idea for you to do that anyway.

LIVE IN THE LIGHT OF GOD'S LOVE—

There is nothing that would make a home a better place to live than to live in the light of God's love: to constantly see something valuable and precious about that person to whom you are married; to constantly see something valuable and precious about those children in your home. God will show it to you. Remember that God sees them that way.

Accept yourself as valuable and precious in God's eyes. Accept yourself as valuable in God's eyes because He sees you that way. Return that love to Him. See Him as valuable and precious, then it will be easier to turn that same love to others in your family.

THE HOPE OF THE WORLD —

If *we* as Christians can't do something about our homes, if *we* can't do something about our families, if *we* can't keep our homes together, if *we* can't keep our families together, if *we* can't make our homes and our families what they ought to be — then nobody can. I really mean that. *We are the hope of the world, "the salt of the earth, the light of the world"* (Matthew 5:13-16).

If God is in your home, there is love in your home. Take full advantage of it. Not for yourself, but in showing it to those other members in your home, for all the world to see.

LET'S HAVE AGAPE LOVE IN THE HOME — AGAPE. That's what love really is.

For more on this vital subject

be sure to pick up a copy of

Dr. Ken Stewart's

HOW YOU CAN HAVE A

CHRISTIAN HOME

also published by Harrison House